MORE
Quickie
COMEBACKS

Lisa Eisenberg and Katy Hall
Illustrated by John DeVore

SCHOLASTIC INC.
New York Toronto London Auckland Sydney

ISBN 0-590-47296-8

Copyright © 1994 by Lisa Eisenberg and Katy Hall. Illustrations copyright © 1994 by Scholastic Inc. All rights reserved. Published by Scholastic Inc.

12 11 10 9 8 7 6 5   5 6 7 8 9/9

Printed in the U.S.A.   01

First Scholastic printing, May 1994

MORE QUICKIE COMEBACKS

It's Monday morning. You're lying in bed, snuggling with your blankie, happily cutting some Z's. What happens next? What *always* happens! Someone comes in and *asks you a stupid question!!* This time, let's say, it's your mom. And she says, "Haven't you gotten out of bed yet?"

Oh, puh-leeeze! Give you a break! Cut you some slack! How are you supposed to answer a question like this? Are you supposed to say, "No, Mom. As you see, I'm still right here in my bed"? Or, "Sorry, Mom. I think I forgot to set my alarm"? No *way!* What you need here is an able answer . . . a clever quip. In other words, what you need here is a Quickie Comeback!!!

In this book, we will take you through the typical day of an average, downtrodden kid — like yourself. We'll cheerfully remind you of all the moronic, nauseating, idiotic questions you're likely to be asked from dawn to dusk, morning, noon, and night — like all day long. But we won't stop with the moronic, nauseating, idiotic questions. Right here, between the covers of this book, we give you the same *power* that you'd get if you crossed a crab and a math teacher — in other words, SNAPPY ANSWERS!

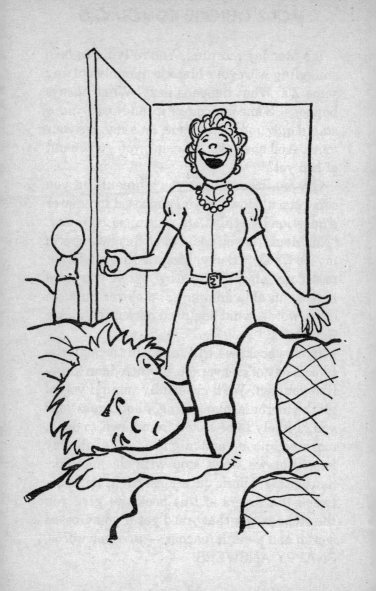

Mother: Haven't you gotten out of bed yet?
Quickie Comebacks:

- Yes, but it exhausted me so much, I got right back in!
- Actually, I *am* up! I'm already on my way to school. The person you see in my bed is really my *evil twin!*
- Why should I get out of bed? In fourteen hours, you'll just make me get back in again!
- *I've* been out of bed for hours! But *you're* still asleep. You're just *dreaming* that you see me here!

Sister: Are you waiting to use the bathroom?
Quickie Comebacks:
- No, I'm modeling my bathrobe for all the pedestrians in our upstairs hallway!
- No, I'm waiting for *you* to use the bathroom. As soon as you go in there, I'm going to sneak into your room and steal your new Madonna CD!
- No, I'm waiting to use the *kitchen*. But the wallpaper pattern is prettier up here!
- No, I'm waiting for a train to Hollywood. I'm going to star in a toothpaste commercial!

Father: Your room looks as if it hasn't been straightened up in a hundred years! Do you call this place *clean?*

Quickie Comebacks:

- No, I call it Fred. It gets angry if I call it anything else!
- Don't blame me! I've only lived here for ten years!
- No, I call it a castle. But then, I'm dangerously insane!
- No, I can't call it at all, because *you* won't let me have my own phone!

Brother: Are you doing your homework *now?*

Quickie Comebacks:

- No, I'm doing it yesterday. You've traveled backward in time.
- No, I'm writing a novel. It's about a boy who strangles his big brother!
- No, I'm just adding up how many times you've poked your nose into my business!
- No, I'm doing *your* homework now. First-grade math is so much easier than what *I'm* supposed to be doing!

Father: Did you comb your hair this morning?

Quickie Comebacks:

- No. I don't want to have smooth hair because then everything would slip my mind!
- Yes, but I combed it with my toes because you told me to try to make both ends meet!

QUICKIE COMEBACKS
ON THE WAY TO SCHOOL

Once you've cleverly quipped your way out of the house, you'll have to deal with all the dumb questions people will ask you on your way to school. Whether you're a walker or a bus rider, believe us, the idiotic inquiries will follow you along your way.

What can you do about it? Well, in the past, all you could do was silently shrug your shoulders, or quietly cross your eyeballs. But from now on, your lips can be armed! Just memorize the following pages of Moving Mouth-offs!

Neighbor: Are you on your way to school?

Quickie Comebacks:

- No, I'm on my way *home* from school! Our new hours are from 1:30 A.M. to 7:30 A.M.!
- Actually, I'm a vampire, and I'm hurrying home to get back into my coffin before the sun comes up!
- No, I'm on my way to *your house.* Do you have any milk and cookies?
- No, I'm running away from home. I've packed my lunch box with enough food to last me for an *entire year!*

Dog Walker: You're not scared of dogs, are you?

Quickie Comebacks:

- That's a *dog?* I thought it was an alligator wearing stilts!
- No, I love dogs. It's dogs' *teeth* I'm scared of!
- No, I'm just scared of *your* dog!
- No, I think your dog is just like a member of your family — *you!*

Fellow Student: Wow, did you drop your notebook and stuff?

Quickie Comebacks:

- No, I *threw* it down here to give myself the chance to do some deep knee-bend exercises! One, two, three, one, two, three!
- No, this is my favorite place for doing my homework!
- No, I've decided to brighten up the neighborhood by decorating the curb with old pieces of notebook paper!
- No, I'm down here because I'm interviewing a family of bugs who live in the crack in the sidewalk!

Passerby: Is this your school bus?
Quickie Comebacks:
- No, it's my family's car. And my mom's the old woman who lived in a shoe!
- Actually, it's the school district's school bus. If it were mine, I'd paint it pink!
- No, it's my rock band's tour bus. Haven't you ever heard of us? We're Shortie and the Ninety-three Elves!
- No, it's a spaceship cleverly disguised as a school bus by aliens who are trying to take over our world!

New Passenger: Are there any seats in the back of this bus?

Quickie Comebacks:

- Yes, but people are sitting in them!
- Yes, but they're under *other people!*
- Yes. We're just standing up because we're planning to have a dance in the aisle!

Bus Driver: Can't you kids keep it down back there?

Quickie Comebacks:

- No! But we sure can keep it *up!*
- We're trying! *Very* trying!
- Keep it down? You mean the bus is floating away again?
- You think *this* is bad? You should hear us in math class!

School Secretary: Good morning! Are all you students ready to learn the three R's: reading, writing, and 'rithmetic?

Quickie Comebacks:

- Not really, but the teacher will probably try to teach them to us anyway.
- No, we're all ready to learn the other three R's: recess, recess, and recess.
- No, we're ready to learn the three G's: going to lunch, going crazy, and going home!
- No, we're ready to *teach* the three R's: resting, resisting, and more resting!

Teacher: Is it raining out?

Quickie Comebacks:

- No, I decided to take a shower with my clothes on this morning!
- No, I jumped into a puddle on the way to school so I could be more like you — *all wet!*
- No, my backpack caught fire on my way to school, and the fire company had to hose me down!
- No, I'm just sweating very heavily!

FROM THE BOTTOM
OF OUR MAILBAG

No matter how many times we move, our fans keep tracking us down and sending us letters. And what's in those letters, you ask? What a stupid question! And that's exactly what's in those letters: STUPID QUESTIONS!

Naturally, given our busy lives, we don't have time to answer each and every stupid question from the many readers of our many books. But we do have our own not-so-stupid question for you: ARE YOU READING THIS BOOK?

Anyway, since Oprah canceled and Donahue booked a serial killer and Sally Jessy said, "We'll be in touch," and even Regis and Kathy Lee turned us down, we don't have anything better to do, so we've decided to write answers to some of these annoying letters. So sit back and enjoy these specimens scraped from the Bottom of Our Mailbag.

dear Katy and Lisa,
I want to become a champion
ski jumper. Do you think there
is any future in it?

Sincerely,
Ian Flyte

Dear Ian,
Frankly, we think jumping
over your skis is about
the stupidest sport we've
ever heard of! Why don't
you take up something
a little more intelligent—
like jumping to
conclusions!

Katy and Lisa

Dear Katy and Lisa,
We want to be writers in
the worst way. What should
we do?
    Teddy and Jimmy A. Brake.

Dear Teddy and Jimmy,
For Pete's sake! Why don't
you want to be writers
in the best way? Like
us, for instance?

        Katy and Lisa

Dear Katy and Lisa,

I'm so interesting, intelligent, and smart, I'm thinking of going to a mind reader. What do you think?

Best Wishes,
Rita Mynde

Dear Rita,

We try to always say exactly what's on our minds and frankly, we're speechless! But anyway, we feel anyone who reads a mind like yours should only charge you half price!

Katy and Lisa

Dear Katy and Lisa

My name is Boris, and I don't have any friends. People tell me it's because I'm so boring. They say I just go on and on about myself and little, uninteresting things about my life, like the time I couldn't sleep one night, so first I went downstairs and got a drink of water, but that didn't work, so then, I tried counting sheep, but that didn't work, so then I put the TV on for a while, but that didn't work, so then...

Dear Boris,
Excuse _us_! We hate to break in like this, but would you mind waking us up when you're finished? Also, we have the solution to your sleeping problem. Just try talking to yourself for a few minutes!!!
Good night,
Katy and Lisa

QUICKIE COMEBACKS
IN THE HALLWAY

Okay, you've arrived at school, and you're ready to go to class. Right? Wrong! First, you have to walk down the hallway and maybe even get your stuff out of your locker. And naturally, as you make your way through the building, you'll be pestered by pinheads pelting you with dumb questions. Don't take it lying down! Be ready with the following Corridor Comebacks!

Friend: Is that your locker?

Quickie Comebacks:

- No, I'm a dangerous peanut-butter-and-jelly-sandwich burglar, and this is where I hide my stash!
- No, it's *your* locker. I just opened it for you to make your life a little easier!
- No — it's the library. Now please shut up so I can study!
- Did you say lock*her*? Obviously, you are a retro-sexist, lacking in political correctness. It's my lock*him*.

Fellow Student: Is this the line for the drinking fountain?

Quickie Comebacks:

- No, it's the line for the mini-hot tub. Where's your suit?
- No, it's a chorus line, and we're the Rockettes. One, two, three, kick!
- Yes! And we're all so excited! We can't wait to see a fountain that can drink!
- No, it's the line to see the assistant principal who's *disguised* himself as a drinking fountain!

Here are some witty remarks useful for making your way through hallways filled with witless questioners!

When you're going up the stairs, and someone asks: How's everything going?
You say: Things are looking up!

When you're headed *down* the stairs, and someone asks: How are you?
You say: I'm feeling a little down!

When you're going into geography class, and someone asks: What class is this?
You say: How in the *world* should I know?

When you're going into math class, and someone asks: What class is this?
You say: Don't *count* on *me* to tell you!

Fellow Student: Did you fall down?
Quickie Comebacks:
- No, I fell *up*. But after I hit the ceiling, I ended up down here again!
- No, I'm meditating in between classes! Ohhhhhmmmmmm.
- No, I'm sitting down so I can sing a lullaby to my toe!
- No, I thought this crowded hallway was the perfect place to practice my forward roll!

TALKING BACK TO THE NURSE

If you're like most of our readers, the first thing you do upon arriving at school is to rush to the nurse's office and claim to be sick. It's a great plan, but, unfortunately, after your seventeenth visit in two weeks, the nurse may start to doubt your word. What will she do at that point? You guessed it! She'll begin asking you a bunch of dumb questions! The only good thing about that is that by the time she's finished, you really will be sick!

Our prescription? Never step through the nurse's door without being ready to needle her with the following set of Sickly Snapbacks.

Nurse: Have you been feeling rundown?

Ill Bill: Only when I cross the street!

Nurse: How did you get that splinter in your finger?

Pale Gale: I scratched my head!

Nurse: If your temperature is normal, I'm going to send you back to class. Is there anything else you'd like?

Sick Nick: Yes! A second opinion!

Nurse: How do you feel today?

Woozy Suzy: Same as always. With my hands!

Nurse: Do you have a cold?

Quickie Comebacks:

- No, I dyed my nose red so I'd look more like my idol — Rudolph!
- No, I just got a part in *Snow White and the Seven Dwarfs,* and I'm Sneezy!

Nurse: What's *your* latest excuse?

Weak Monique: I think I'm a bird!

Nurse: That's ridiculous! I'm sending you to the principal's office!

Weak Monique: Aww, is that any way to tweet a person?

Nurse: Why are you in here today?

Weak Monique: I think I'm a bee!

Nurse: That's the worst yet. Get out of my office right now!

Weak Monique: Are you telling me to buzz off?

Nurse: Okay, let's hear it.

Dizzy Lizzy: I think I'm a strawberry!

Nurse: Do you expect me to believe that? Get back to class right now!

Dizzy Lizzy: Oh, great. Now I'm really in a jam!

Nurse: This is the last time I'm going to listen to one of your fake illnesses.

Woozy Suzy: But I feel like a bathtub!

Nurse: You're driving me crazy! Get out of here and don't come back!

Woozy Suzy: Okay. Should I give you a ring in an hour or so?

COMEBACKS WITH CLASS

You've tried everything to get out of it. But somehow, in spite of your best desperate efforts, you've ended up in the classroom anyway. And it's time to face the truth. You are right smack in the middle of the Capital of Cloddish Questions. If ever you needed a load of Quickie Comebacks, the time is now! So stand up and talk back! (And then get your hall pass to the principal's office!)

Teacher: Are you late *again?*

Quickie Comebacks:

- No, I'm right on time. The rest of you were early!
- No, I'm way ahead of time — for tomorrow's class!
- No, I'm afraid I'm a little ahead of schedule. I was trying not to get here till recess started!
- Yes, that's me. Late again. I don't see how you can stand to have such a student in your classroom, so farewell, *adios,* good-bye, I'm outta here!

Teacher: Did your parents help you with your homework?

Quickie Comebacks:

- No, I got it wrong all by myself!
- No, my parents *harmed* me with my homework!
- Absolutely not. *Nobody* did my homework!
- I asked them, but my father said it wouldn't be right. I told him he could at least give it a *try!*

Teacher: Are you listening to music during my class?

Quickie Comebacks:

- No! My ears are dirty, and I'm using these headphones to cover them up!
- No! These are my new over-the-head barrettes!
- No! I'm listening to instructions from the aliens who bolted these transmitters onto my skull!

Teacher: Is everyone looking forward to taking the big test this afternoon?

Quickie Comebacks:

- Yes, and after that we're looking forward to walking over a bed of sharp, pointy nails!
- No, I'm looking forward to going home sick this afternoon!
- No, I'm looking *sideways* to the test this afternoon — sideways to the class brain's paper!

Teacher: Do you want to know why I gave you a D on your science report?

Quickie Comebacks:

- Because my name is Durwood?
- Because D stands for "Duh"?
- Yes! I thought I was going to get an F!
- Oh, it was supposed to be a *science* report?

Teacher: Class! Class! Can we have order in here please?

Quickie Comebacks:

- All right! I'll have a large Coke, fries, and a cheeseburger!
- Okay. I'll leave first, he'll leave second, she'll leave third!
- No, but if I were a skunk, we could have some *odor* in here!
- You asked for it. On your feet! Face the door. And, march, two-three-four!

Teacher: Who can spell Tennessee?
Quickie Comebacks:
- Presumably, *you* can!
- One-a-see, two-a-see, three-a-see . . .

CAFETERIA COMEBACKS

You and your quick tongue have survived stupid questions all morning long. By now, you're feeling pretty tough. But if you have to put up with cafeteria queries from cutups who talk with their mouths full of macaroni, well, it could pretty much make you lose your appetite, or even make you toss your tacos all over that freshly mopped cafeteria floor. So — you guessed it! On the upcoming pages you'll find a colossal compendium of Cafeteria Comebacks!

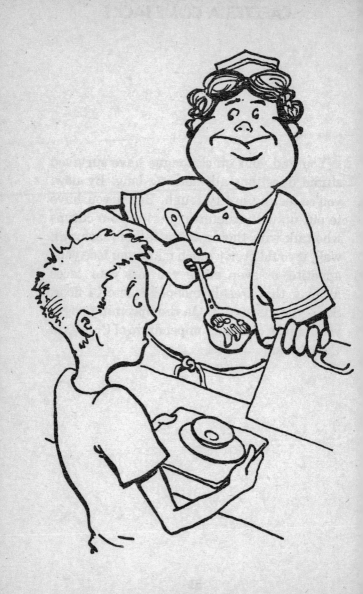

Cafeteria Worker: Are you having lunch today?

Quickie Comebacks:

- You mean I don't *have* to?
- Gee, I don't know. I just thought I'd stand here in line with my tray and see what happened.
- No, this is my breakfast. I got up at eleven!
- No, I just came from English class where there was enough food for thought to last me the rest of the day!

Cafeteria Worker: Have you tried our beanie-weenie casserole?

Quickie Comebacks:

- No, which is why you see me here before you, alive and well!
- No, have *you?*
- Not since I got out of the hospital!
- No, I just became a serious vegetarian!

Nosy Neighbor Nora: Are you going to eat those fish sticks?

Quickie Comebacks:

- I was, but I heard you've been collecting them since first grade, so here, have mine!
- No, I'm going to play pickup sticks with them. C'mon, it's your turn!
- Yes, before they have a chance to eat me!
- No, I'm going to *stick* them into my ears so I won't have to listen to any more of your fishy questions!

Chuckie: Is that your slice of pizza?

Quickie Comebacks:

- No, it's your slice of pizza that hopped onto my plate and begged me to eat it!
- Yes, it is, and if you ask me any more questions, I'll give you a pizza my mind!

Betty Burp: How come you didn't finish all your coleslaw?

Quickie Comebacks:

- I only like *hot* slaw.
- 'Cause it's about to finish me!
- Because if the head of cabbage that it came from is anything like *your* head, it's totally rotten!

Monique Monitor: What's the matter, don't you want to be in the Clean Plate Club?

Quickie Comebacks:

- Gee, I don't know. How often does it meet?
- Nah, I'm a member of the Disgustingly Dirty Plate Club.
- Not me, but could my dog become a member?

RECESS RIDICULE

Once you've brilliantly blabbed your way through a morning in the classroom and come out on top with the lunchroom loonies, you'll undoubtedly be thrown outside and told to exercise something besides your mouth. You *might* think that, out on the playground, you'd be safe from silly questions. But you'd be wrong! Swings, slides, and basketball hoops are not protection against Ridiculous Recess Requests. Save yourself by running through the following reams of Recess One-liner Retorts.

Margery: Do you like to go on the seesaw?
Quickie Comebacks:
- Well, it has its ups and downs!
- No, it makes me feel unbalanced.
- No! And if you *saw* what I *see* — your face! — you wouldn't have to ask.

pet rock.

Sandy: Do you like to play in the sandbox?
Quickie Comebacks:
- Yeah, man, I can really dig it!
- No, I just can't *sand* it!
- No, it always makes me feel a little *pail*.

Sadie Sue: Are you waiting to use this slide?

Quickie Comebacks:

- No, standing in line is my new hobby.
- No, I'm a chicken, and I want to get to the *other* slide!
- No, I'm waiting to see the doctor — to ask him why you'd ask me such a silly question!

Bunny: Do you like to play hopscotch?
Quickie Comebacks:
- No, but I make myself do it for at least two hours a day because I think it improves my ability to read the numbers from one to ten upside down.
- No, I always chalk it up as a loss!
- Yes, because it makes me so hoppy!

LIBRARY LAST LAUGHERS —
A QUICKIE COMEBACK STORY

At some point during your typical, idiotic-inquiry-infested day, you'll probably end up in the library. Even though people are supposed to be quiet in libraries, you still won't be safe there. Somehow, somewhere, when you least expect it, someone will shower you with stupid questions.

How can you fight back? Get the word by reading up on the following Library Last Laugher Story.

Librarian: Do you realize just how overdue this book is?

Boy: Yes, but it's a math book, and I just couldn't bear to return it till I'd helped it solve some of its problems!

Librarian: Why, you've had this book for more than six months! Do you know how I feel about students who have overdue books?

Girl: Just *fine!*

Librarian: Shhhhh! What a racket! Don't you know the other people in here can't read?

Girl: Why, that's terrible! I've been reading since I was six!

Librarian: Do you *have* to make so much noise?

Boy: I'm sorry, but I can't help it! It's a cookbook, and it's just so *stirring!*

Librarian: Are you planning to return those books any sooner than you did the last ones?

Boy: Oh, no. I have to start practicing for my future career. I'm planning to become a *bookkeeper!*

I SHOULD TRY NOT TO GET MAD AT YOU KIDS TODAY. AFTER ALL, IT'S BE KIND TO ANIMALS WEEK.

WHY DON'T YOU ALL GO TELL YOUR TEACHER SHE WANTS YOU?

OR GO OVER TO THE ZOO AND TELL THE KEEPER YOU'RE HOME?

I NEVER FORGET A FACE, BUT FOR YOU KIDS, I'D LIKE TO MAKE AN EXCEPTION.

DO OTHER PEOPLE IN YOUR FAMILIES SUFFER FROM INSANITY? OR DO THEY ENJOY IT?

DID YOU HEAR THE ONE THAT GOES: WHAT DID THE LIBRARIAN SAY TO THE BOOK? MAY I TAKE YOU OUT TONIGHT?

THE ARTFUL COMEBACK

Whether it's drawing or sculpting or our specialty — finger painting! — sitting in an art class gives the artist working next to you the perfect opportunity to ask you all those things that are on his mind. Fortunately for you, if the artist sitting next to you is anything like the bozo who sat next to us, there isn't that much on his mind. Hardly anything at all. But that's never stopped anyone from asking away. That's why we're presenting you with our Artful Advice on Artistic Answers!

Artie: So, how do you like my work of art?
Quickie Comebacks:
- Anyone could tell that you're its father.
- I only wish I'd seen it before lunch. I'm dieting and it would have killed my appetite.
- How could you stand to look in the mirror long enough to do a complete self-portrait?

Artie: Duh, what is that?

Quickie Comebacks:

- A blunt instrument.
- A sharp instrument.
- Maybe a little birdie will tell you — but I won't!
- Actually, it's an I.Q. test and if you can't tell, I guess you didn't pass.

SCHOOL'S OUT-RAGEOUS COMEBACKS!

You thought that three-thirty bell would never ring. But at last, school's over for the day and you're free to — hit the ground for forty push-ups or maybe the gym floor for one hundred sit-ups — all in the name of after-school sports.

Well, you can be a good sport only for so long. Whether your game is volleyball, basketball, football, tennis, or Ping-Pong, there are bound to be coaches and fellow team players who ask questions that are clearly out of bounds. That's why we give you now our Sporty Little Responses.

Losey Lucy: Is that a football?

Quickie Comebacks:

- No, it's a handball.
- No, it's a secret guided missile that is attracted to hot air, so you'd better close your mouth.

Coach: Do you call yourselves a basketball team?

Quickie Comebacks:

* Yes, and our team name is the Dribbling Disasters!
* No, we only call ourselves for dinner.
* No, *you* call us a basketball team.
* No, we call ourselves human beings. What should we call you?
* Right! We're the Dream Team — your worst nightmare!

Willy Watcher: Are you playing baseball?
Quickie Comebacks:
- No, I just carry this mitt around in case I see any butterflies.
- No, I'm just wearing a great big pot holder.
- No, I'm trying to catch flies because I'm a spider!

Willy Watcher: Why are you just sitting on the bench?
Quickie Comebacks:
- 'Cause I'm a chicken, and I was thrown out of the game for using fowl language!
- 'Cause I'm Dracula, the batboy!
- 'Cause I'm so nice, I'd never even hit a fly!

Wally Watcher: Are you a cheerleader?

Quickie Comebacks:

- No, I'm participating in a scientific experiment to test the strength of pom-poms by seeing how long they will last with me waving them around.
- Right. Just call me Old Yeller.
- No, I'm a member of the team but they ran out of uniforms.

Once your after-school sports team has admitted defeat — and why is it that a winner like you is always on the losing team? — it's time to scurry on home to hit the books. The only problems you might encounter here are your mom, dad, sisters, brothers, cousins, friends, slight acquaintances, and even parakeets who want to ask you what you're doing. As we always say when people ask us too many questions, "What's that? I can't hear you. I have a banana in my ear!"

Unfortunately, we usually get hungry and eat the banana and then the peel turns all black and icky and keeps slipping out of our ear and then we hear all those horrible, horrendous, harping harangues about our homework. To save you the trouble of buying bananas (and even of *going* bananas) we've home-worked out some Pretty Smart Remarks!

Sissy: Aren't you finished with your homework yet?

Quickie Comebacks:

- Yes, I'm just doing next month's homework ahead of time.
- No, the teacher assigned us to write about a member of our family. I chose you, and it took me a long time to look up the words *moronic, nauseating,* and *idiotic.*
- No, I'm working on my master plan to become an only child!
- Yes, I finished hours ago and now I'm watching TV. Why do you ask? Are you having hallucinations or what?

Mad Dad: How could you get an F on your
  science test?

Quickie Comebacks:

• The girl I used to copy off of moved away.

• No problem. It's those A's that are a little
  tricky.

Big Bro: Hey, what's all this stuff?

You: My history report.

Big Bro: I know it's your history report. How stupid do you think I am?

Quickie Comebacks:

- Do you really want me to answer that question?
- Oh, somewhere between a pet gerbil and a pet rock.

Momsey: Oh, no. Your homework is spread out all over the kitchen table again. How many times have I told you not to do that?

Quickie Comebacks:

- Oh, about as many times as we've had hamburger surprise for dinner.
- I don't know. I haven't learned numbers that big yet.
- Your guess is as good as mine.
- I don't know, but when a gong sounds, we'll know you've hit the one million mark!

MEALTIME MEANIE-MOUTHIES

Even while you're eating, the people in your family will hurl horribly hackneyed questions at you until you're ready to throw up your hands — not to mention your food! So, now's the time to talk with your mouth full of Mealtime Meanies.

Dad: Don't you like your peas?
Quickie Comebacks:
- Oh, I love my peas — so much, I want to use them as marbles at recess tomorrow!
- Yes, I like them. But my *tongue* hates them!
- Yes! I like them too much to torture them by eating them!
- No. *Peas* don't make me eat them!

Mom: Would you like some rare roast beef?
Quickie Comebacks:
- Sure! Pleased to *meat* you!
- No! I prefer getting my blood supply directly out of my victims' necks!
- Do you think you could cook it a little longer? I could swear I just heard something say, "Moo!"

Sister: Do you want your dessert?
Quickie Comebacks:
- No, I want *your* dessert!
- Not really. But we just ran out of those delicious Brussels sprouts, so I guess I'll be forced to eat this hot fudge sundae instead!
- Yes! And if you think you're getting your hands on it, you'll find out who put the *scream* in *ice cream*!

SWEET DREAMS
OF SWEET RETORTS

After swallowing as much hamburger surprise as you could stomach for dinner — and letting Fido sit under the table and eat the rest out of your napkin — you're ready for a little R & R. Rest and relaxation? No way. At your house, R & R can only mean one thing (okay, two things): Respond and Reply. And why is that? Because no one in your whole family knows when to say *when* when it comes to ASKING STUPID QUESTIONS!

But, hey! Armed with our handy-dandy comeback *TV Guide,* you can put those snoopers in their places with our Remote Retorts!

Tiny Tina: Are you watching *I Dream of Jeannie*?

Quickie Comebacks:

- No, I'm watching *I Scream of Jeannie*, and if you don't zip it up, I'll be screaming at you!
- Yes. What a *genie*-us you are to figure that out!

Sister Kate: Oh, are we bothering you?

Quickie Comebacks:

- No. I didn't really want to watch my favorite show tonight anyway. I'd much rather hear all the details of how your geeky friends were dressed for the dance!

- Of course not! Please, don't stop talking or I'll never know whether Bobby has green eyes or brown!

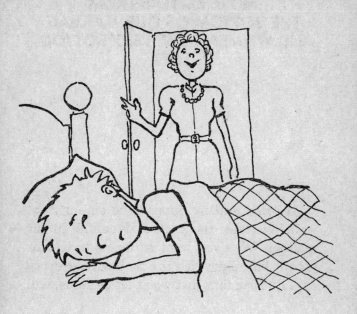

Mom: Psst! Are you asleep?
Quickie Comebacks:
- No, I'm just using my head to hold my pillow down so it won't float up to the ceiling.
- No, I'm reading the inside of my eyelids.
- No, I always find it restful to lie in bed with my eyes closed and pretend to be sleeping.

WHAT???
MORE LETTERS FROM
THE BOTTOM OF OUR MAILBAG
AND WE MEAN THE *VERY* BOTTOM,
TOO

We tried putting Super Glue on our front walk. We tried the stick of dynamite in our mailbox. We even went so far as to let our pet pit bull play with the mail carrier every day. But you fans just won't let us alone, will you?

What do we have to do to get you to quit shipping us your mail bags of moronic questions? Answer your letters? Will *that* stop you?

Hmmm. Come to think of it, maybe it will. In fact, now that you mention it, our fans who get *our* nasty answers never ever write us back again! (Sometimes their lawyers do, but never the fans.) So, read the next few pages and help us in our campaign to stamp out our fan mail forever!

Dear Katy and Lisa,
I have an appointment to get my head X-rayed next week, and I'm very nervous, what should I do?
Noah Little

Dear Noah,
Don't worry! We're sure the X ray of your head will show absolutely nothing! You can head off to your appointment with a _really_ clear mind!
Katy and Lisa

Dear Katy and Lisa,
My little brother follows me and does exactly what I do all the time. It drives me crazy. How can I solve this problem?
Lee Veemalone

Dear Lee,
Tell your little brother to stop acting like an idiot!
Katy and Lisa

Dear Katy and Lisa,

all my friends say i'm really stupid just because in math class, when my teacher started telling us about a polygon, I thought she was talking about a lost parrot. I don't think this is so dumb, do you?

Io Wanda Know

Dear I. Wanda,

Noooo, we don't think it's one bit stupid. But then, we think Sean Penn is a prison for bad actors!

Katy and Lisa

Dear Katy and Lisa

I skipped gym class the other day and my team lost the soccer game. Now my coach wants to know why I wasn't there. What should I tell him?

Jim Cutter

Dear Jim,

Just tell Coach that you don't get a kick out of soccer.

Katy and Lisa